INSPIRATION

Inspiration

PAUL CHENEOUR

Redgoldmusic.com

Contents

Dedication vi

Inspiration 1

About The Author 20

To all those on the
	path

Copyright © 2023 by Paul Cheneour

All rights reserved. No part of this book may be reproduced in any manner whatsoever without written permission except in the case of brief quotations embodied in critical articles and reviews.

First Printing, 2023

Inspiration

In the slipstream

The Dervish whirls and whirls
Being everything and nothing
Arriving everywhere and nowhere
Such is the bliss in the beloved
Such is the ecstasy in the divine dance
Spin
Turn
Spin
Feet no longer touching the ground

Leaving Silently
Slipping past the door
A half eaten morsel of bread
Only here am I nourished
Then filled I notice
It was you all along

From afar
See me come running
Behind those eyes
You changed me
Behind your eyes
You changed

Intoxicated life
Standing between two worlds
I am drunk with this breathing
My dance never stops
Both of us entwined here
With something important
Then I had to slip away

An elegant being
Beyond light and dark
With settled heart
Only hears clarity
And simplicity
In the flute notes

Out across the valley
Walking through rain
A fragrant passion wafts
Through imaginary halls
Illuminating dimly lit rooms
No arriving
No leaving
No arriving
No leaving

Stop running after approval
Equations are delusions
Dressed as fact
Reason laughs at us both
As we sit here
In this reality mine field
Emotionally naked
Be centred and listen

In the fading light Nasrudin says
Hatred is not compulsory
The silent tsunami of
Thoughtless words
Wash over us
Gently untie your bindings
Be free from sorrows and
Dream like an Egyptian
I cannot believe it is not napalm

Porcelain skin
Pale blue eyes singing
Silent love songs
Reaching out across the years
Souls bound together
We are almost lovers
But not quite
Best to part quietly
And leave it there

Leave your ideas
And wantings behind
Move across the doorsill
Put on white robes
Dance in the freezing sunrise
Be a Fusionista
No hiding from this
Incomparable beauty

Did you buy the lie
Stop your weeping
Open the window
In your chest
And let love fly in and out
You are so full of treasures
In this art of madness

Inward outward
Inward outward
Always active
Claiming lives
Let go of
Elation and dissolution
Agony and ecstasy
Be motionless
In this moving moment

Way of Waiting

Learn the way of waiting
The silent ticking
Of mortality through
Shifting sands
Of careless words
Sharpen your senses
Fear is no longer legal tender
Or a currency accepted here

A new passion descends
Time for the great ending
The turning circle is complete
Be open to fresh thinking
Embrace a new radical enterprise

Stop your weeping
Change everything
Arrive at nothing
Listen to the language of birds
Tell your own stories
About this duopoly game
Remember how
It feels to be you

Down in the Valley
Scented air floats towards
An opening in the veil
Soul breathes in
Then sighs as it
Looks at you and asks
What are you really doing

Glistening sunrise
Frost covered thoughts
Snow covered actions
A dancing nymph
Embraces the fire dragon
A beautiful thawing occurs

Blazing Nights
We are strangers
Under the night sky
With fire in our souls
Beyond those two imposters
Light and dark
The time for fence sitting
Is over

Run between the raindrops
Move silently
Leave no footprints
A message from water
Is asking
Why do you come here

Climbing uphill
Closed doors swing open
The hurting heart
Turns towards love
Fall into that place
Where everything is music
Savour the joy of disappointment
And raise yourself again
Like a Phoenix

Fire walking
Where have you been
Be still in the storm of the eye
The Guardians of this Earth
Are waiting outside
To ensure your roasting

See with clarity
Loosen the knots of your robe
Join the Matzoobs
Those crazy wisdom people
Move beyond cleverness and trickery
Leave complexities behind
It is all
As it is

Quietness
Am I too loud
Shush
Too loud
Am I still too loud
Shush still too loud

Passing over
The veil between worlds
Is gossamer thin
To move between them
Simply snap your fingers
Eternity is held in a moment
Do not squander your time
In useless pursuits

Watching the symphony body
Listless in summer heat
Tired in winters chill
Witness the rising and falling
Am I still too loud
Shush still too loud

Wordless words
Amble arbul orible
Bramble barble bearable
Canker collapse grimace
Damsel demolition finish
Does my small voice
Still trouble you

Inside Solitude
Meandering into twilight
Somewhere between
Dream and reality
The demolition orchestra
Is painting wonderous pictures
In sound just for you

Turning inwards
The Sandgate sadhu says
There is a wonderous
Beauty coming
But first we must wait for the
Time Weaver to appear
Until then we keep turning

If an equation
Equals delusion
Does something
Plus nothing
Equal everything
Change everything
And arrive at no thing
Are we sleepwalking
Our way towards
Bullshit Bingo

Foreboding skies outside
Torrential rain inside
Who are the profiteers from this doom
Is it those green eyed dragon people
Or the handmade purple people
From the box of Pandora
Am I still too loud
Shush
Still too loud

Who looks out from my eyes
Stop your weaving and
See how the patterns grow
Soar like an untethered kite
Consult the thirteen moon calendar
And become a gardener
Of your own beauty

After the long farewell
Meditate on the corrosive system
Keep walking Zen flutes of the west
Be disobedient
Refuse to submit
To the gulag of servitude
Nasrudin says
It is the system that is insane

Way of Being

Dawn is coming
The Visionistas are
Leaving by the back door
Their job is done
But only
For the time being

Silent portraits writhing
Birds perched eager to fly
Through mountain mists
Swirling winds
Wandering haphazardly
In carved out canyons
Waiting for possibilities

We are strangers
Laying here in a silent stupor
In this back alley room
Covered by ancient sands
Wake your dulled senses
Begin walking that road
To your own remembrance

The fine line
Between
Nocebo
Negative words
And balanced simplicity
Is exquisite instinct

Fana is an expression
Of incomparable beauty
Broken open in the dance
Fix your gaze
Upon the beloved
And turn

Call me again tomorrow
At this moment
I am in conference with the birds
Suitably dressed in red robes
With a great sydhu
Locked in ecstatic communion
Seeing with clear eyes

Inscriptions abound
His Infernal Slyness
Has spoken of the great reset
Hatred is no longer compulsory
There is an error in time
We are calling for a
Genuine rehabilitation

Morning Comes
See how you have grown
Tell us of your adventures
And how they feel
The fast train is speeding
Towards our destiny
Do tell us another Nasrudin story

Stand Alone
Stop your nonsense
End your slavery
Run with the wind
Lift your heart
Above the blazing cacophony
And shout your uniqueness
Into the ear

Shimmering sun
Shines on the sea
Through a haze of
Slash and burn
Organise a revolution
Wind up the World Bank
Corporates are not allowed here

Forgiveness
Like a red sky at night
Is full of hope
Sing quadrilles to the stars
With unconditional love

Leave no trace
Mithra god of truth
Only sees poverty
In the midst of plenty
Oh yes
What is this farcical
Free trade agenda
Thing anyway

Sounding forth
The night gardener
Does not shy away from
Being an imaginer
In the highest realms
Creating existence
From a single note

In the early hours
Making ready for departure
Is it time to solve
The goldilocks enigma
With the karma police.
Or is it just another
Omnishambles

Radiate silently outwards
Remain stylistically neutral
Sin palabras
Without words
Be a quantum activist.

Arriving without moving
In the soft twilight
Portland Bill chain man
Slips through rocky outcrops
Meditating on expressions
Of self and non self

Into the unknown
Beyond the beyond
Enter a tea shop at noon
Where Harry the Headache
Is celebrating
Courtesy kindness and consideration
Are the only means of exchange here

Green

Feelings of Green
Between lines drawn in sand
Softly hear the call
Turn your face towards the sun
Forget the grains of time passing

Seasoning
A continuous movement
Adding flavours
Turning
Churning
Stirring
Always something new
Moving through lives
Fragments barely noticed
Our enrichment is simmering
In this living cooking pot

Cork Tree
Expands with fire
Keeps wine imprisoned
Drinking only sunlight and rain
Dancing in its own delight

Is this Paradiso
I enter a grey town
Turn a cobbled corner
A sudden image flashes
A memory jolted
Have I played here before

Tranquility
I tried to find you
Amongst the screaming
Where were you hiding
I searched in all the wrong places
All along you were there
Beside me

A warm heart
Savours each moment
Tracing paths in time
Races with anxiety
Fending off darkness
With love

A fair trade
What are we exchanging
Do not use a proxy
Step cautiously across
The bridge that joins us
This trade today
Is full and fair

There are shining lights
Looking skywards
From the beach
Faces are turned
Towards the beyond
Aware of earths spiral trajectory
A glowing essence reaches down
And gently touches me
On the cheek

Forever faithful
Each time I arrive here
A new body
A new life
A new learning
Being separated
From the ocean is pain
Trying always to be true
This is all I can do
Over and over
And over again

Run with the wind
Child of the land
Do not be bound
Loose all restrictions
Have no fear
Run I say
Run towards yourself
Sublime revelations
Are coming
And very soon

Night Mist

Night mist
Has secrets to tell
Memories
Of forgotten deeds
Of excited possibilities
Yearning to be heard
Catch those whispers
Before they
Disappear forever

Ceremonial
Procession
Moving
Slowly forward
Together in unity

Watching fire
Cleaning the body
Softened by
The intermediary
Of water

The Seer
Remains silent
Waiting
For the right
Question

Willow Shadow
Meets sunlight
On the ground
Diffused
By fountain spray
I am just
A raggedy nothing

Red Castle
Entertains guests
With wine
With music
With hidden delights

Lakeside
Murmuring lilies
Stretched out across
Carpets of fire
Enticing fairies
To dance with fevered
Abandonment

Envoys Path
Is often
A lonely road
Towards reconciliation
With ourselves

When we were silent
A warm embrace
A loving smile
A gentle touch
There are many ways
To show compassion

Gathering Clans
Coming together
In a sacred space
Infused with the
Essence of glorious
Celebration

The end of sorrows
An unexpected
Gift arrives
And fills you
With an exquisite
Tenderness

Paul Cheneour has walked a broader musical path throughout his career embracing European Classical, Jazz, Arab, Indian, Celtic, and other music's, culminating in his own 'World Fusion' style.

"Tapping into the source of creativity takes great courage and even greater competence in acquired skills.
Paul Cheneour, a leading UK jazz, classical and ethnic flautist/composer suffered a near fatal car crash in '91.

He recovered with the conviction that he needed to use his talent, life, and near-death experience to explore a new forms of creative expression. This amounts to an opening out to the influences available in the moment.

All the world's great musical and artistic traditions remain as resources and are no longer seen as restrictive boundaries"

(Interview extract by Michael Greevis for Colour Therapy Magazine UK. 1995)

www.ingramcontent.com/pod-product-compliance
Lightning Source LLC
Chambersburg PA
CBHW021135080526
44587CB00012B/1300